By Jacquie Tyre

The Jabez

PRAYER GUIDE

A
Personal
Journey to
God's
Blessing

A *Pray!* Magazine Book

Pray! Books • P.O. Box 35004 • Colorado Springs, Colorado 80935 • www.praymag.com

Words of Gratitude

My deepest gratitude goes to the following people, with much love:

My husband, Mike, and our three sons, Aaron, Nathan, and Justin. Thank you for supporting me and loving me through times of joy, sorrow, victory, and defeat. In many ways the very writing of this book comes as the fruit of God's dealings with me through our journey together as a family. You are the best!

My parents, Wade and Charlotte Johnson, who have given me unconditional love, challenged me to aim higher, and encouraged me to pursue God's best all my life. Thank you for just being you—faithful, loving parents and servants of the Most High God. You've taught me more than you will ever know.

Pastor Fred Hartley and the congregation of Lilburn Alliance Church. You have each contributed in special ways to the development of my life and this prayer guide. If not for our Lord using you to encourage, challenge, and give opportunity for these prayer guides to be used, this day would not be here. May God's hand continue to be upon you to the praise of His holy name.

Jonathan Graf and the staff of *Pray!* and *Pray!*Books for seeing God's hand upon this work and investing in seeing this book come to completion. May God bless you, indeed!

Most of all, my deepest thanks and love goes to the Lord Jesus Christ, for without Him no blessings would exist. He is not only the Bless-er, but the Blessing!

Dedication

I would like to dedicate this book to the loving memory of three very special people who went to be with the Lord within the past year:

My grandmother, Roma Thomas, affectionately known as MawMaw. When I was a child, she and Papa allowed me to learn the joys of serving the Lord by their side whenever I visited them. What a marvelous heritage!

My dear friend, Robin Askins, who died of breast cancer in May 2000. Robin lived life to its fullest until the very last minute. In reflection, she lived out the prayer of Jabez daily. Her life challenged me to press forward and to not settle for mediocrity in anything! Her friendship was truly a blessing from the Lord.

Finally, Armin Gesswein, the great statesman of the prayer movement and a man I was privileged to have touch my life for the last seven years through Prayer Summits and the College of Prayer. God used him to speak blessings and challenges that remain dear to my heart.

—Jacquie Tyre

Foreword

You are holding in your hands a dangerous little book about a dangerous little prayer. Right now it is in the process of changing my life; it can change your life as well.

I pastor a church in metro Atlanta that is becoming a house of prayer for all nations. We adopted the prayer of Jabez as our year verse and asked Jacquie Tyre to write a supplemental prayer guide that was first published for our congregation. It struck a chord. More and more people began asking for copies until now it has found its way into your hands.

Over the next few weeks as you put these pages to good use, I want to issue a warning. This dangerous little prayer is not a magical formula or a good luck charm. Bottom line, it's not the prayer of Jabez we need; it is the God of Jabez. I and my congregation are praying for you and yours that He will show you just what a dangerous, not-so-little God He really is.

Fred A. Hartley III
Senior Pastor, Lilburn Alliance Church
Lilburn, Georgia
June 2001

How to Use This Guide

The Jabez Prayer Guide is simple in format, but powerful in results if a few instructions are followed.

1. Don't take shortcuts. The real strength of this *Guide* lies in what you glean and pray related to the Scriptures. Read all of the scripture suggested with each day.

2. Turn the Scriptures into prayer. Suggestions on what to pray are provided each day. We recommend that you turn some of the thoughts from the Word you read into your prayers.

3. Stay the course. Pray through the entire *Guide,* If you miss some days, pick it up where you left off. The whole of this *Guide* provides a real cross section of important issues on which to seek God.

4. Pray this for more than yourself. This *Guide* is designed to be used by the individual. But we recommend praying these blessings for your family, friends, and your church. In fact, many churches are using this *Guide* corporately, with every member praying it at the same time.

"Lord, Bless Me Indeed"

> *"And Jabez called on the God of Israel saying, 'Oh, that You would bless me indeed, and enlarge my territory, that Your hand would be with me, and that You would keep me from evil, that I may not cause pain!' So God granted him what he requested."*
>
> (1 Chron. 4:10, NKJV)

We know very little about Jabez from Scripture, except that he was more honorable than his brothers and that his mother named him Jabez because she bore him in pain (the Hebrew word for pain sounds like Jabez)(1 Chron. 4:9). But while we know little about what Jabez *did*, we can understand much from what he *prayed*.

There is nothing to indicate he made this request because he believed he deserved it more or thought he was better than anyone else. Jabez simply recognized his need and voiced it before God. He needed God to bless him and he dared to ask, not having any idea how God would answer the bold request.

We know that God did answer Jabez. Does that mean God wants *us* to ask Him for blessing? Absolutely! Our God is all good and He delights in responding to His children when they ask Him in faith and boldness to meet their needs.

Jabez, whose name was pain, cried out to the Lord for a release of heaven on earth! Jesus taught His disciples to pray, "Your kingdom come, your will be done on earth as it is in heaven" (Mt. 6:10)—a model of asking for God's blessing, indeed.

Have you identified your deepest needs and desires? Are you convinced of your absolute need for God to bless you? Then believe God to release a touch of heaven's aroma into your life. Expect Him to reveal more of Himself in you.

Lord, bless me indeed. Let Your kingdom come to bear upon me so that Your goodness and glory are realized and revealed in greater measures in and through me. For Your Name's sake. Amen.

ʃ∪ℵⷧ∀ℽ: Lord, is it okay to pray like this?

"Lord, bless me." Does this prayer make you uncomfortable? Does it seem somehow too self-centered? Would you feel more at ease praying for others? If so, you are not alone. God's word, however, clearly says that it is wise to desire God's blessing—and to ask Him for it. In Genesis 32, Jacob wrestled with the angel of the Lord and cried out: "I will not let you go unless you bless me!" Not only was his prayer answered, but Jacob is honored for all eternity for his tenacity and desperate desire to receive the blessing of God.

Scripture: Read Genesis 32:22-32.

Prayer: If you need to, confess your hesitancy to pray this prayer. Then by faith, boldly pray, "Lord, bless me indeed!"

Reflections: _____

_____

_____

_____

_____

_____

Mⷩℵⷧ∀ℽ: The Covenant Blessings of God

The Hebrew word for bless is *barak* (*Strong's Concordance* 1288). It means to "kneel down, salute, congratulate, praise, or thank." Our God is a God of blessing. All blessings originate with Him, and blessings were a significant part of His covenants with man through Abraham, Isaac, and Jacob. God's ultimate covenant with us—the Lord Jesus Christ—establishes us to receive His blessings for all eternity. In Christ, He has been delighted to give us all we need for life and godliness (2 Pet. 1:2-4).

Scripture: Read the original blessing covenants: with Abraham (Gen. 12:1-3, 22:15-18); with Isaac (Gen. 26:1-6); and with Jacob (Gen. 28:13-15).

Prayer: Ask God to grant you the grace to understand and lay hold of all that He has given you in Christ Jesus, blessing you freely, so that through you, others may be blessed.

Reflections: _____

_____

_____

_____

_____

TUESDAY: Positioned to Receive

A covenant is a binding agreement between two parties, based upon a mutual commitment to each other, for a specified purpose. Covenants require the satisfaction of conditions for fulfillment. God is a covenant-keeping God. Our part of the "conditions for fulfillment" are that we join Him by faithfulness and obedience to His Word. This positions us to receive His blessings, which are ours by covenant.

Scripture: Read Deut. 30:11-20; Lev. 26:18-19; Psalm 1. Note the connection between God's blessing and His requirements for receiving the fullness of those blessings.

Prayer: Ask the Holy Spirit to lead you in repentance and a fresh commitment to walk in the ways of the Lord, positioning you to receive His blessings.

Reflections:

WEDNESDAY: Ask and You Shall Receive

"You do not have because you do not ask. You ask and do not receive, because you ask amiss, that you may spend it on your pleasures" (Jas. 4:2-3, NKJV). God desires that we ask. And He promises to give, if we ask according to His will (1 Jn. 5:14) and in the Name of the Lord Jesus Christ (Jn. 15:16), and are abiding in Him (Jn. 15:7) so that His desires become ours (Ps. 37:4). He wants to bless us with every good and perfect gift (Jas. 1:17-18), so that through His children of promise all the nations of the earth might be blessed (Gen. 12:1-3).

Scripture: Read Mt. 7:7-12.

Prayer: Ask the Lord to forgive you for not asking, or for asking amiss. Ask Him to search your heart and reveal the places where your will does not line up with His. Ask Him to purify your motives. Then ask Him to bless you so you might receive every good and perfect gift from Him and become a blessing to those around you.

Reflections:

THURSDAY: That They May Be One

"How good and pleasant it is when brothers live together in unity. . . . For there the LORD bestows his blessing, even life forevermore" (Psalm 133). God delights in pouring out the blessings of abundant life upon His children who dwell together in unity. These verses seem to suggest that unity is needed for God's blessing to come. Our unity greatly pleases Him—it is like "precious oil poured on the head" (Ps. 133:2), because it bears testimony to His love. That unity is what Jesus asked on our behalf when He prayed to the Father: "May they be brought to complete unity to let the world know that you sent me and have loved them even as you have loved me" (Jn. 17:23).

Scripture: Read Psalm 133; Jn. 17:20-26; Eph. 4:3.

Prayer: Repent before God for any areas of isolationism, prejudice, pride, or separation that keep you from walking in unity with fellow believers. Cry out to God for purification of yourself and the church in this area. Ask the Holy Spirit to guide all believers to keep the unity of the Spirit through the bond of peace.

Reflections:

FRIDAY: The Promised Holy Spirit

Jesus said, "I am going to send you what my Father has promised; but stay in the city until you have been clothed with power from on high" (Lk. 24:49). It is by the power of the promised Holy Spirit dwelling in us that we are able to lay hold of all the blessings God intended for our good. Jesus promised us the Holy Spirit to empower us as effective witnesses to the world of His grace, mercy, life, love, power, and salvation. The Lord desires to fill *each of us* with this most precious gift.

Scripture: Read Acts 1:4-8, 2:1-4.

Prayer: Seek the Lord for a fresh filling of His Holy Spirit and receive it, by faith, with gratitude. Ask for opportunities to bless others, allowing the Holy Spirit to minister the grace of the Lord through you. Ask specifically for the blessing of salvation upon two or three people who need it.

Reflections:

SATURDAY: Lord, Bless Me Indeed

Our Father has promised to bless us. He *has* blessed us. And it is His desire to continually bless us. His blessings on our lives flow through us and reveal Him to the world around us. As Jabez did, we can expect God's blessings to come to us. We can expect that we will receive much, and that God's Name will be exalted and glorified through those blessings.

Scripture: Read Psalm 21.

Prayer: Thank God for the blessings you have already received, and for those you have not yet received or recognized. Praise the Lord that He is our ultimate blessing and our primary reward.

Reflections:

"Enlarge My Territory"

> *"And Jabez called on the God of Israel saying, 'Oh, that You would bless me indeed, and enlarge my territory, that Your hand would be with me, and that You would keep me from evil, that I may not cause pain!' So God granted him what he requested."*
>
> (1 Chron. 4:10, NKJV)

Jabez asked God to bless him—bless him *indeed*. He didn't want an obscure or unidentifiable blessing. He wanted God's blessing upon his life to be a sure thing—a real deed. So Jabez got *specific*.

The first specific Jabez asked for was: "God, enlarge my territory." Increase my realm of service, my influence, my authority. Expand the boundaries of my inheritance. By virtue of God's covenants with His people, Jabez knew there was potential for increase that he did not yet have. He wanted all God had for him, so he was bold in his request. In that request, we hear a holy dissatisfaction with his life. Something was lacking. Jabez knew it, and he chose to do something about it—he asked God!

If we are going to pursue the full blessings of God, we need to understand and align ourselves with God's *purposes* for blessing. First, as a good Father, God loves to bless us (Mt. 7:9-11). He delights in bestowing His best upon us. Second, it is God's will that all the people of the world receive blessing through His people (Gen. 22:15-18). So He blesses His children to enable us to be distributors and conduits of His blessing to the rest of the world.

Asking for such blessings might seem prideful to some. But it is more your expressing faith in the God who promised to "do exceedingly abundantly above all that [you can] ask or think" (Eph. 3:20, KJV).

This week ask the Lord to broaden your vision, extend your faith, expand your prayers, and enlarge your capacity to love so that through you others might be blessed with the revelation of Jesus Christ as Savior, Lord, Redeemer, Healer, and Deliverer.

Lord, I know You delight in blessing Your children. Teach me about Your blessings so that I might walk in them, and therefore bless others, for Your Name's sake and for Your glory.

SUNDAY: Do I have a territory?

Before we can ask the Lord to enlarge our territory, we must first be aware that we have received one. Territory is that portion of inheritance given to every saint of God, promised and granted by covenant. It is a place of privilege as well as responsibility. In essence, territory encompasses your sphere of influence. It can include your family, business, neighborhood, community, and ministry. Regardless of the size of your territory, God has given it to you for a purpose—a purpose that abounds with blessing

Scripture: Read Deut. 11:18-32.

Prayer: Ask God to enable you to receive with gladness the territory He has given you. Thank Him for each individual and aspect of responsibility that is within your area of influence. Repent, if necessary, for the ways you may have neglected to care for or occupy your territory. Ask God for grace to responsibly occupy all that He has given you thus far.

Reflections:

MONDAY: What does God require of me?

God gives us territory. It is ours by birthright—either natural or spiritual. However, we must possess it, just as Joshua and the Israelites did in the land of Canaan. Part of possessing our territory lies simply in asking God for what He has promised. The other part, however, rests in obedience to His Word and commands.

Scripture: Read Deut. 1:6-8, 31:1-13.

Prayer: Pray earnestly today regarding promised territory that God would have you possess. Ask Him to reveal it to you, and enable you to lay hold of it through faith, diligence, and prayer.

Reflections:

TUESDAY: Now what? The enemy is here!

When God gives us a place of service and influence, we often discover that the enemy meets us there. He mounts an attack, trying to get us to turn back and give up the very territory God has said we are to possess. The Israelites had to fight the occupants of Canaan in order to possess the land. So we, too, must "evict" the enemy of our souls in order to occupy the promised territory. We do it with the weapons God has given us—submission to God, the sword of the Spirit, prayer, praise, worship, and endurance—remembering that the Lord Jesus Christ has defeated the enemy already.

Scripture: Read Ro. 16:20; Eph. 6:10-18; Jas. 4:7-10.

Prayer: Spend time today asking the Lord for His strategy to evict the enemy from your territory. Ask for grace to answer those who oppose you. Pray that God's peace would rule and reign in your heart (Phil. 4:5-9). Pray this for yourself and for your church.

Reflections:

WEDNESDAY: From Possessing to Abiding

God grants us territory so that we might abide in His presence, in the center of His good pleasure and purpose for us. This is the place of blessing, for it is in abiding that He has ordained that we will be fruitful and multiply. When we abide in Christ, we will automatically abide in the place of our God-given territory.

Scripture: Read Jn. 15:1-17.

Prayer: Pray through Jn. 15:1-17. Respond to God's Word however He leads you—in confession, repentance, supplication, gratitude, or intercession. Ask God to settle you into a place of abiding and release the blessing of fruitfulness, for His glory.

Reflections:

THURSDAY: Lord, there must be more!

You find yourself in a place of blessing and fruitfulness, living in the territory God has given you. Nevertheless, something within you begins to rumble—a yearning to reach more people, expand the scope of God's blessings through your life. Is this selfish, egocentric, prideful? Not necessarily. Jabez asked for more, and God granted his request. It all depends on the motivation of your heart. Is it pure before the Lord? This is the key to having God answer the prayer to enlarge your territory.

Scripture: Read Ps. 139:23-24; Jer. 17:9-10; Jas. 4:3; 1 Jn. 5:14-15.

Prayer: Ask the Lord to search your heart and to purify your innermost motivations. If He reveals impure motives, repent. Ask God to transform you from the inside out, so that He might be pleased to enlarge your territory.

Reflections: _____

_____

_____

_____

_____

FRIDAY: Lord, enlarge my territory!

Your desire is to bless. You are willing to take the risks and pay the price to possess what God has for you. You want what God wants, above all else. Now the bold prayer can rise upon your lips, assured that God wants to grant you your request. He simply has been waiting for you to come into alignment with His Word and ask in faith.

Scripture: Read Mk. 11:24; Phil. 3:12-16; Heb. 11:6; Jas. 1:6.

Prayer: Boldly ask the Lord to enlarge your territory and increase your service, ministry, influence, and authority. Ask for grace to walk in trustworthiness over all that He has set apart for you. Ask that your life will bless many as His blessings flow to you and through you.

Reflections: _____

_____

_____

_____

_____

SATURDAY: You, O Lord, are so good to me!

The Lord knows our every strength and weakness, and He alone knows how best to use us. He knows where our boundaries should be set. As the psalmist declares: "LORD, you have assigned me my portion and my cup; you have made my lot secure. The boundary lines have fallen for me in pleasant places; surely I have a delightful inheritance" (Ps. 16:5-6).

Scripture: Read Ps. 16:5-11.

Prayer: Spend today thanking, praising, and worshiping God for His goodness and generosity.

Reflections:

"That Your Hand Would Be with Me"

"And Jabez called on the God of Israel saying, 'Oh, that You would bless me indeed, and enlarge my territory, that Your hand would be with me, and that You would keep me from evil, that I may not cause pain!' So God granted him what he requested."

(1 Chron. 4:10, NKJV)

Bold prayers for blessing and enlarging of territory, birthed out of this little verse, fill the heavens and thrill the heart of our Father God. He is looking for people who yearn to walk in a greater measure of what He has promised, and who are willing to ask for it, boldly and expectantly. He is looking for people who will ask and then receive, responding responsibly and obediently to all that He gives.

The next part of Jabez's prayer presses a little further, expressing a deep desire for something beyond what God can give him. Jabez cried out to the Lord that His "hand would be with him." He was no longer asking only for what God's hand held; he was asking for the reality of His hand—His touch, His favor. Jabez wanted God's presence, not just His presents.

In order to understand what we really are asking for in this portion of the prayer, we will take a scriptural journey into the effects of God's hand upon His people. Ask the Holy Spirit to give "you the spirit of wisdom and revelation in the knowledge of Him," and that "the eyes of your understanding being enlightened; that you may know what is the hope of His calling, what are the riches of the glory of His inheritance in the saints, and what is the exceeding greatness of His power toward us who believe" (Eph 1:17-19, NKJV).

Lord, I ask with faith for the manifestation of all that You have promised to Your children. Lead me to my inheritance in You. Grant it Lord, according to Your will.

SUNDAY: The Hand of Righteousness

God is altogether righteous, and His hand, therefore, is full of righteousness. It stretches out with full evidence of His nature. "Like your name, O God, your praise reaches to the ends of the earth; your right hand is filled with righteousness" (Ps. 48:10). When the hand of the Lord rests upon a person, it brings righteousness and justice to bear upon that life, for He delights in dwelling with His children in those ways.

Scripture: Read Hos. 14:9.

Prayer: Tell the Lord about your desire for His righteous hand to be with you, to rest upon you, to transform you more and more into His likeness. Ask the Lord to give you an understanding of the holy and righteous aspects of His character.

Reflections:

MONDAY: The Hand of Conviction

In remembering days of conviction that led to repentance, the psalmist said, "For day and night your hand was heavy upon me; my strength was sapped as in the heat of summer" (Ps. 32:4-5). Part of the reality of God's hand is its weightiness against all that is *not* holy. The heaviness of His presence convicts us of sin, righteousness, and the judgment to come. To ask for the hand of the Lord to be with us is to invite His convicting power to invade our lives—which is good, needful, and greatly to be desired.

Scripture: Read Psalms 38 and 39.

Prayer: Ask today for God's heavy hand of conviction to search your life. Respond in humility, contrition, and repentance to His convicting touch. Receive His forgiveness and cleansing (1 Jn. 1:9) and ask for grace to gain victory in the confessed areas.

Reflections:

TUESDAY: The Hand that Saves

The Lord's hand saves us from our sin, redeeming us by the great mercies of our God. Day by day and moment by moment, we need His saving hand to hold us, and to stretch out to rescue us when we stray. He wants to save us—even when we seem beyond saving—and He *can*: His arm is not too short to save and His ear is not too dull to hear!

Scripture: Read Ps. 17:6-8, Ps. 20:6; Is. 59:1.

Prayer: Offer prayers of thanksgiving for the saving hand of the Lord, and ask Him to hold you safe and secure all your days. Pray for His hand to stretch out and save those who seem far away from His grace.

Reflections:

_____

_____

_____

_____

_____

_____

_____

WEDNESDAY: The Hand that Restores

The blessings of restoration come directly from the hand of the Lord. Restoration involves renewal, return, and repair: "I will restore to you the years that the swarming locust has eaten" (Joel 2:25, NKJV). It also means to make something live again or to set it up again. Isn't it good to know that when the hand of the Lord comes to convict us of sin, it also comes to save and restore us?

Scripture: Read Ps. 23:3, 80:7-19; Is. 57:16-18.

Prayer: Ask the Lord to bring restoration to your life—specifically in areas where you have suffered loss, either through personal sin or circumstances that took something away (health, relationship, provision, etc).

Reflections:

_____

_____

_____

_____

_____

_____

THURSDAY: The Hand that Undergirds

After God saves and restores, He holds us up. A connection exists between the expansion of our territory and the undergirding hand of the Lord. When He expands our territory, we must have His hand holding us up—for it is not by our own strength that we press forward, but by His. Notice the connection between God's sustaining hand and the enlargement of the psalmist's path in today's Scripture.

Scripture: Read Ps. 18:35-36.

Prayer: Ask the Lord to undergird you as you walk into the territory that He opens before you. Confess those times when you have tried to walk in your own strength and have not recognized your absolute dependence upon God.

Reflections:

FRIDAY: The Hand that Defends

God is mighty and strong, a defender of the humble, and a protector of the weak. When we are oppressed by evil, or helpless in fear, or weakened by sadness, we call out to God: "Arise, O LORD! O God, lift up your hand! Do not forget the humble" (Ps. 10:12, NKJV). He will listen, and encourage, and defend "in order that man, who is of the earth, may terrify no more" (Ps. 10:18).

Scripture: Read Psalm 10.

Prayer: Confess your need for the Lord's defense against the assault of wickedness both through temptation and oppression. Cry out for God's defending hand to be with you, to protect and deliver you from the oppression of wickedness.

Reflections:

SATURDAY: The Good Hand of the Lord

Numerous times in Ezra and Nehemiah, we read variations of the phrase, "according to the good hand of the Lord that was upon me." Each time this phrase was spoken, it referred to the fact that the hand of God had granted favor and blessing. His hand had provided all that was needed for the enormous tasks that were before Ezra and Nehemiah. We might call this the hand of favor, or grace, or anointing, or blessing. When we go into challenging situations—be it in our family, on the job, or in the ministry—we need the good hand of the Lord upon us.

Scripture: Read Ezra 7:6,9,28, 8:18,22,31; and Neh. 2:8,18.

Prayer: Ask the Lord for the blessing of His hand upon you, granting all you need in the territory He has given. Seek His grace to continue to occupy the territory He enlarges for you. Ask that it may be done to the praise and glory of His name, that His kingdom might be expanded throughout all the earth.

Reflections:

"That You Would Keep Me from Evil"

> *"And Jabez called on the God of Israel saying, 'Oh, that You would bless me indeed, and enlarge my territory, that Your hand would be with me, and that You would keep me from evil, that I may not cause pain!' So God granted him what he requested."*
>
> (1 Chron. 4:10, NKJV)

Jabez probably knew more about pain than most. His mother named him Jabez "because (she) bore him in pain" (1 Chron. 4:9). Yet, somehow Jabez must have tapped into a well of hope, because he gained a mention in the Holy Scriptures as a man who was "more honorable than his brothers." What was it about Jabez that had such distinction?

According to *Strong's Exhaustive Concordance and Dictionary*, the Hebrew word for honorable, *kabad* (#3513), means "to be heavy, make weighty, be glorious." These words are usually associated with the Lord God Himself. He alone is all-glorious and full of honor. The presence of the Lord, His glory, is weighty and great. There is nothing else like it. Therefore, a person who is considered honorable is one who bears a resemblance to the Lord, bearing the honor of His character in purity, humility, and passion.

Jabez knew that apart from God he was destined for nothing but pain—to cause pain and to experience pain. This destiny may well have made him a man with a broken and a contrite spirit—one whom the Lord would not despise (Ps 51:17). Jabez knew that there would be nothing for him outside of the Lord's provision, direction, and protection. So he cried out, "keep me from evil." He recognized the evil crouching at his door, and he cried desperately for God's protection: Keep me from evil. Do not let me stumble in sin. Protect me from the evil one. Guard my heart. Watch over my ways.

In order to pray "keep me from evil" with integrity, we must acknowledge our own propensity to go the way of evil, the way of sin. For if we don't understand the desperate condition of our own heart, we cannot fully grasp the power and impact of God's protection.

Lord, grant me in humility a deep revelation of the sinful condition of my heart. Lead me to walk in the place You've provided for protection from evil.

ṢUNḐAY: God Provides a Way

Praying that the Lord would keep us from evil does *not* mean that we will not face temptation. Even Jesus, though He was without sin, experienced temptation (Heb. 4:15). God's Word to us, however, declares that He will not allow us to be tempted beyond what we can handle, and He provides us a way out.

Scripture: Read 1 Cor. 10:13.

Prayer: Ask the Lord to deliver you from any misconceptions you might have about what it means to pray, "Lord keep me from evil." Ask for faith to face temptation and go the way of escape that the Lord provides to keep you from evil.

Reflections:

_____

_____

_____

_____

_____

_____

MONḐAY: Kept from Evil by Doing Well

"Your adversary the devil walks about like a roaring lion, seeking whom he may devour" (1 Pet. 5:8, NKJV). The adversary looks for specific places to enter our lives. We must allow the Lord Jesus Christ—our Protector from evil—to take dominion over those "entrances." In Him, we have strength to do what is right, which enables us to rule over temptation and resist the sin that lurks at the door of our hearts.

Scripture: Read Gen. 4:7.

Prayer: Ask the Lord to show you any doors in your life where sin lies in wait, looking for an opportunity to overtake you. Repent and ask the Lord for grace to reposition yourself in obedience to "do well" and be accepted.

Reflections:

_____

_____

_____

_____

_____

TUESDAY: Kept from Evil by Abiding

"If you make the Most High your dwelling—even the LORD, who is my refuge—then no harm [evil] will befall you, no disaster will come near your tent. For he will command his angels concerning you to guard you in all your ways" (Ps. 91:9-11). This entire Psalm contains wonderful promises and instructions for being kept from evil. All of them have to do with abiding in Him: dwelling with Him in the secret place (intimacy in prayer), and resting in the shadow of the Almighty (surrender and consecration), loving Him, and calling on Him.

Scripture: Read Psalm 91.

Prayer: Pray through Psalm 91, expressing to God your own desire and need to abide with Him. Claim His promises to protect you from evil. Acknowledge your commitment to dwell in the secret place of prayer with Him and to surrender to Him under His Almighty shadow.

Reflections:
_____
_____
_____
_____
_____

WEDNESDAY: Kept from Evil by Prayer

"Give ear to my words, O LORD, consider my meditation. Give heed to the voice of my cry, my King and my God, for to You will I pray. . . . You are not a God who takes pleasure in wickedness, nor shall evil dwell with You" (Ps. 5:1,4, NKJV). Prayer connects us with the Almighty, tapping us into His provision by acknowledging our dependency and letting our requests be known. Evil cannot dwell with Him; so evil cannot grab hold of us when we dwell in His presence.

Scripture: Read Psalm 5.

Prayer: Pray through all of Psalm 5, personalizing it for your life and situation. Ask God to show you any places in your life where you have been guilty of prayerlessness or self-reliance and repent of those.

Reflections:
_____
_____
_____
_____
_____

THURSDAY: Kept from Evil by Seeking Good

"Hate what is evil; cling to what is good. . . . be wise about what is good, and innocent about what is evil. The God of peace will soon crush Satan under your feet" (Ro. 12:9, 16:19-21). When we are consciously looking for good and intentionally avoiding evil, God will establish new things in us that transform our lives, and keep us from evil.

Scripture: Read Amos 5:14-15; Phil. 4:8-9.

Prayer: Ask the Holy Spirit to search your heart and reveal any place where you are not living under the influence of these verses in Amos, Romans, and Philippians. Repent and commit yourself to look for good consciously and hate evil intentionally. Consider attitudes, possessions, entertainment, conversation, social practices, and your leisure time.

Reflections:

FRIDAY: Kept from Evil by Holiness

"Let us cleanse ourselves from all filthiness of the flesh and spirit, perfecting holiness in the fear of God" (2 Cor. 7:1, NKJV). Holiness, according to *Spirit-filled Life Bible*, is separation from everything profane and defiling while at the same time, dedication to everything holy and pure. When we set ourselves apart to walk in His way, the Lord puts us on a path where evil cannot tread.

Scripture: Read Psalm 51; Is. 35:8-9.

Prayer: Offer prayers of consecration and sanctification, asking the Lord to set you apart for His purposes and therefore keep you from evil.

Reflections:

SATURDAY: Kept from Evil by Praise

When the people of Israel praised the Lord as they marched into battle, He set ambushes against their enemies (2 Chron. 20:21-22)! When we give ourselves to praising the Lord God Almighty at all times and in every situation, we can often see evil defeated before our eyes. Remember that "the battle is not yours, but God's" (v. 15). He is well able to keep you from evil.

Scripture: Read 2 Chron. 20:1-30.

Prayer: Praise the Lord specifically over any situation you face that looks impossible or looks as is if evil is about to win. Watch for the ambushes He sets against evil as you praise Him.

Reflections:

"That I May Not Cause Pain"

> *"And Jabez called on the God of Israel saying, 'Oh, that You would bless me indeed, and enlarge my territory, that Your hand would be with me, and that You would keep me from evil, that I may not cause pain!' So God granted him what he requested."*
>
> (1 Chron. 4:10, NKJV)

Jabez cried out to the Lord: "Bless me. Enlarge my territory. Let Your hand be with me. Keep me from evil." Why? "So that I may not cause pain!" Jabez did not want God's blessing to end with him. He wanted to see goodness flow through his life.

Jabez knew that God's blessings could reverse the curse of pain, grief, and sorrow in his own life. He knew that increased territory would enable him to bless others in greater measure. He knew that God's hand would lead and uphold him. And, he knew that God's protection from the assault of evil was his only hope and way of escape—both from his own suffering and from causing pain to others.

If, as you've meditated upon and prayed Jabez's prayer, you've struggled with its focus on self, "that I may not cause pain" is the phrase that can set you at ease. The Jabez prayer does cry out for God's blessing on our lives. But the plea is not for selfish gain or personal advancement. Ultimately, the cry of the prayer is that others might be blessed through our lives.

There are areas where we, as believers, have the potential to cause others pain. Our loving God, however, desires to bring blessing to all of mankind through His children. It is from His heart that this phrase of Jabez's prayer arises.

Lord, I know You want me to be a blessing to others, and not to cause them pain. Search my heart and attitudes, Lord, and reveal the ways of pain from which I need to be set free.

SUNDAY: May I Not Cause Pain by Anger

Interestingly enough, the Hebrew word for pain in this verse can also mean anger. One way we can hurt others is through intermittent outbursts or ongoing behaviors that are rooted in anger. Often our anger will lash out in response to something (or someone) that offends, hurts, or threatens us. Sometimes anger flares in a situation that reminds us—consciously or unconsciously—of hurt or damage from the past.

Scripture: Read Gal. 5:16-26.

Prayer: Pray through the Galatians passage, asking the Lord to bring healing and deliverance to your heart in any area of unresolved anger. Repent and release forgiveness where needed. Ask for His Spirit of forgiveness, mercy, gentleness, and kindness to flow through you and be a blessing to others.

Reflections:

MONDAY: May I Not Cause Pain by Betrayal

God created us with an internal need for safety and security in relationships. Whenever a trust or covenant—either clearly stated or implied—is breached or broken between people, feelings of betrayal can ensue. Betrayal might take the form of "bailing out" on a relationship, misleading others by stretching the truth, inappropriate disclosure of personal information, or outright deception.

Scripture: Read Col. 3:12-17.

Prayer: Ask the Lord to search your heart for areas where you may have caused suffering through acts of betrayal, or where you have been betrayed. Repent and seek reconciliation or restoration in those relationships. Ask the Lord God to heal the wounds in you and others, and to enable you to avoid wounding others through betrayal in the future.

Reflections:

TUESDAY: May I Not Cause Pain by Rejection

Rejection is defined as refusal to "take, use, believe in, accept, acknowledge, hear, consider, or grant" something. It can also mean to "throw away as useless or unsatisfactory" or to "rebuff" something. By these definitions, we have all both suffered rejection and inflicted rejection on others. Consider this amazing thought: Jesus Christ suffered *rejection* ("refused" or not "believed in") for us so that we might find *acceptance* (worth before God) in Him.

Scripture: Read Eph. 1:3-14.

Prayer: Ask the Holy Spirit to search your heart and reveal times and ways you have suffered rejection and/or inflicted it on others. Respond with prayers of repentance, supplication, and intercession for yourself and others. Rejoice in your acceptance in Christ.

Reflections:

WEDNESDAY: May I Not Cause Pain by Judgment

Christ taught that we are not to judge, lest we be judged. He taught that we should remove the plank from our own eye before we attempt to take the speck out of our brother's eye (Mt. 7:1-5). Often, however, we are guilty of judging harshly and rashly those who do not live according to our standard. Judgment is particularly harmful when we hold it over unbelievers. It may well keep them from seeing and responding to the message of Christ's redeeming love. Many of us also have suffered from having been judged—by the Christian community and by unbelievers alike—and are in need of healing.

Scripture: Read Romans 14.

Prayer: Ask the Lord to heal you from the judgment of others, and receive His mercy. Then, pray for those whom you may have wounded through judgmental attitudes and behaviors. Intercede for the whole church to become more like Christ in mercy, and to be set free from the spirit of judgment and harshness.

Reflections:

THURSDAY: May I Not Cause Pain by Hatred

St. Francis of Assisi prayed, "Where there is hatred, let me sow love." Our world is full of hatred. Hatred is defined as "very strong dislike, loathing, aversion, animosity, ill will." Take a look around you. Where you see hatred, intentionally sow love. If you discover any hints of hatred in your own heart against anything or anyone (other than evil and the enemy), repent. Sow love through prayer over those whom you find it most difficult to love or to like. Dismantle the pain of hatred by purposeful acts of love.

Scripture: Read 1 Jn. 3:10-23.

Prayer: Ask the Lord to show you where you may have caused pain through hatred. Repent of this and ask Him for the grace to sow love where there was hate, especially in the people and situations you find most difficult.

Reflections:

FRIDAY: May I Not Cause Pain by Sin

No man is an island. The consequences of our actions—both good and bad—affect those around us, particularly those closest to us. Choices that give in to temptation and go the way of sin always cause pain. While we cannot undo past choices, we can repent and ask for forgiveness from God and from those we have hurt.

Scripture: Read 1 Jn. 1:5-2:11.

Prayer: Pray Ps. 139:23-24. Where sin has caused pain to you or through you, take it to the cross in prayer. Cry out to God for forgiveness, healing, and restoration. Ask God for His wisdom in how to approach those you've hurt to ask forgiveness.

Reflections:

$ATN R \mathcal{D} A J$: May I Not Cause Pain by _____

The list of things that can cause pain could be an endless one. There may be other issues that cause pain in your life or have led you to cause pain in the lives of others that are not mentioned here. Fill in the blank with what is most significant to you. Remember that a day shall come when God "will wipe every tear" and there will be no more "crying or pain" because we will be living forever in the presence of the Lord.

Scripture: Read Rev. 21:1-5.

Prayer: Ask the Lord to heal your pain, bring restoration to your soul, and set you free from anything in you that might bring others pain. Release prayers of faith and hope as you meditate on Rev. 21:4.

Reflections: _____

_____

_____

_____

_____

_____

_____

"So God Granted Him What He Requested"

> "And Jabez called on the God of Israel saying, 'Oh, that You would bless me indeed, and enlarge my territory, that Your hand would be with me, and that You would keep me from evil, that I may not cause pain!' So God granted him what he requested."
>
> (1 Chron. 4:10, NKJV)

Jabez—a man called pain; a man desperately desiring a new identity; a man who called upon the God of Israel; a man who dared to offer a bold prayer before His Lord; a man who *received what he requested.* Jabez went from being a man of pain to a man of blessing—simply because he faithfully let his request be known to God.

The word from which "granted" is translated is not the one typically used in Hebrew. More often, *nathan* (Strong's 5414) is used—meaning "to deliver, bestow, give forth." In this case, however, the word *bow* (Strong's 935) is used. *Bow* means "to go in, enter into, come upon, or abide." It is often used to indicate God's coming to a particular person or place.

The other key word in the phrase—"requested"—is *shaal* in Hebrew (Strong's 7592). It means "inquired, demanded, asked, begged, consulted, desired earnestly, or prayed." The word implies an intensity of passion in the request. Jabez cried out to God in passion, fervency, and desperation. And God was apparently pleased with his request, because He answered it.

In response to his passionate plea, God did not send an "answer." He came *Himself* to Jabez! No greater blessing can exist.

This is what God most wants to give us—Himself. In order to receive this gift, we need to have our hearts tuned to Him in prayer. Prayer is the primary tool God has given us to commune with Him. He wants to be with us, not just to send us answers and provisions. He *does* send answers and provisions along the way. But the very best answer to any request lies in God coming to us. He fulfills our every need, our every desire, as we delight ourselves in Him (Ps. 37:4).

Lord, lead me to discover the blessings of receiving Your ultimate answer to every prayer: by coming to me that I might abide more fully with You. Allow the blessing of Your presence to flow into me and through me to touch others.

SUNDAY: God of Righteousness

"And the heavens proclaim his righteousness, for God himself is judge" (Ps. 50:6). When God comes to His people, "a fire devours before him and around him a tempest rages" (Ps. 50:3), bringing judgment upon the unrighteous and deliverance and blessing to the faithful. Search your heart. Are you prepared for His appearing? Are you positioned to receive all the Lord desires to give you in blessing?

Scripture: Read Psalm 50.

Prayer: Using Psalm 50, praise God for His all-consuming righteousness. Ask Him to do what's necessary to prepare you for the reality of His presence in your life. Ask Him for grace to seek His face in righteousness, truth, and justice.

Reflections:

MONDAY: God of Holiness

God is holy. His holiness is so profound and complete that it's impossible to be in His presence without acknowledging His beauty—His perfection, splendor, and might. So we are called to worship Him in the beauty of His holiness (Ps. 29:2). When God comes to us in His holiness, He brings the blessings of strength and peace (Ps. 29:11).

Scripture: Read Psalm 29.

Prayer: Pray through the psalm, offering praise, petition, and earnest supplication for Him to come in holiness upon your life, family, and community. Ask for guidance to respond appropriately.

Reflections:

TUESDAY: God of Truth

Like Jabez, the psalmist earnestly sought the Lord: waiting patiently for Him, trusting in His goodness, crying out for His blessings—and God granted his request (Ps. 40:1-3). In the midst of need and oppression, the psalmist remembered that the God of truth does not change and that His truth can always be trusted (vv. 10-11). When God comes to us in truth, we are given a firm place to stand (v. 2).

Scripture: Read Psalm 40; Is. 55:8-13.

Prayer: Ask the Lord to remind you of His truths that apply to your stated need. Pray those truths back to Him—trusting, believing, and expecting Him to grant your request.

Reflections:

WEDNESDAY: God of Peace

Paul wrote that we do not need to be anxious about anything. We can experience God's unfathomable peace by presenting our requests to Him with thanksgiving. God then guards our hearts and minds from the things that distract and harass us.

Scripture: Read Phil. 4:6-9.

Prayer: Ask the Lord to show you any "anxious" areas in your life that you need to release to Him in prayer and thanksgiving. Ask Him to come to you as the God of peace, leading you to His peace that passes understanding. Intercede (stand in the gap) in the same way for someone else who needs peace.

Reflections:

THURSDAY: God of Hope

In Christ Jesus, we are made partakers of divine hope—a hope that endures, a hope that comforts, and a hope that abounds to all who call upon His name. God has provided us with the means of hope through His Word and through the Holy Spirit. We can take every need before the Lord with confidence that He will fill us with His joy and peace.

Scripture: Read Romans 15:1-13.

Prayer: Take your most pressing need to the God of hope. Ask the Holy Spirit to bring scriptures to your remembrance for comfort, instruction, and encouragement. Pray in a like way for someone else who is carrying a heavy burden.

Reflections:

FRIDAY: God of Comfort

"Praise be to the God and Father of our Lord Jesus Christ, the Father of compassion and the God of all comfort, who comforts us in all our troubles" (2 Cor. 1:3-4). Jesus declared that He would send the Comforter or Counselor (the Holy Spirit) to live in us and guide us. God delights in granting our request for the fullness of the Holy Spirit, because it is a "good gift" (see Mt. 7:7-12).

Scripture: Read 2 Cor. 1:3-7.

Prayer: Ask the God of comfort for a fresh filling of the Holy Spirit. Pray that you would receive His comfort and be an instrument of distributing it to others under the power of the Holy Spirit.

Reflections:
_____

_____

_____

_____

SATURDAY: God of Love

God is love. The greatest blessing we can ever receive is Love: God Himself. The God of love manifests Himself in our lives in patience and kindness. He is not found in envy, boasting, rudeness, selfishness, or evil. He causes us to rejoice in truth, bear all things, believe all things, hope all things, and endure all things. He never fails (1 Cor. 13:4-8), and He casts out fear (1 Jn. 4:18). He came to earth to redeem us from sin (Jn. 3:16) and prepare the way for an intimate relationship with Himself.

Scripture: Read 1 Corinthians 13; 1 Jn. 4:7-12.

Prayer: Worship the God of perfect love. Ask Him for a fresh baptism of His love over your life and over others—in your family, your community, and the world.

Reflections:
_____

_____

_____

_____

May the God of love . . . the God of Jabez . . . the God of your heart, soul, mind, and strength . . . grant you what you request.